Hitting, Pitching, and Running–Maybe

Author
Gary Paulsen

Photographer
Heinz Kluetmeier

 RAINTREE EDITIONS

Copyright 1976, Raintree Publishers Limited

1 2 3 4 5 6 7 8 9 0   80 79 78 77 76

Library of Congress Number: 76-18092

Printed in the United States of America

Published by	Raintree Editions, A Division of
Raintree Publishers Limited
Milwaukee, Wisconsin 53203
Distributed by	Childrens Press
1224 West Van Buren Street
Chicago, Illinois 60607

Library of Congress Cataloging in Publication Data

Paulsen, Gary.
    Hitting, pitching, and running—maybe.

    SUMMARY: A humorous commentary on different aspects
of baseball using photographs of professional players.
    1. Baseball—Juvenile literature. [1. Baseball]
I. Kluetmeier, Heinz.   II. Title.
GV867.5.P38   796.357'02'07   76-18092
ISBN 0-8172-0178-5
ISBN 0-8172-0177-7 lib. bdg.

Everybody knows how to play baseball, right?

If you're up, you smash the ball over the fence and make runs.

And if you're not up, you keep the *other* guys from smashing the ball over the fence to make runs.

Well, this is a book on how to do both of these things.

Sort of.

Hitting

Batting is not as easy as you think. You can't just walk up to the plate and smack the ball. First you have to select a bat. Make sure the peeling is off.

Then you have to get into position for batting. This is known as addressing the plate. If you don't address the plate perfectly before batting, it's almost impossible to hit the ball.

After addressing the plate, you have to straighten your batting helmet. Then you have to knock the dirt off your cleats, and make certain that your elbow is low, the bat high, and your stance correct. It helps, however, if you don't try to do all of these things at once.

Then you *swing!* When the ball comes over the plate in the right place. Not too soon. Not too late. If you do it just right, you'll hit a home run every time. But then, nobody can do it right every time.

Pitching

In pitching, probably the most important thing is the windup. It's also a pretty good time to scratch your ankle.

After you finish the windup, you throw the ball across the plate. You try to throw it so the batter can't hit it. If you do it perfectly three times in a row and the umpire isn't mad at you, you'll strike out the batter.

Of course, there are times when things
don't go right and the batter hits the ball.
Hard. Far away.

That's when you need all those other guys on the team—like the ever-alert outfielders. They catch the ball and throw it back to the infield and keep the batter from scoring. Sometimes.

18

Running

The best part of baseball is when you're batting and *you're* the one who hits the ball. Hard. Far away. Then *you* get to make a blur while you run around the bases.

The most important thing to remember about running the bases is not to get caught by anybody with the ball. It helps to look in back once in awhile to see where the ball is.

If the ball is sailing toward the baseman,
you have to think about sliding.
Sometimes the best time to think about
sliding is after it's over, while you're
resting.

If you want to score, you have to remember to touch home plate before the catcher touches *you* with the ball. Sometimes it's close. Even scary.

27

When you do it all right—hit, pitch, and run—you make the fans happy. Which isn't all that hard, because fans are usually happy anyway.

Of course, the fans aren't the *only* ones who get happy. Sometimes the players go crazy, too. Usually when they win.

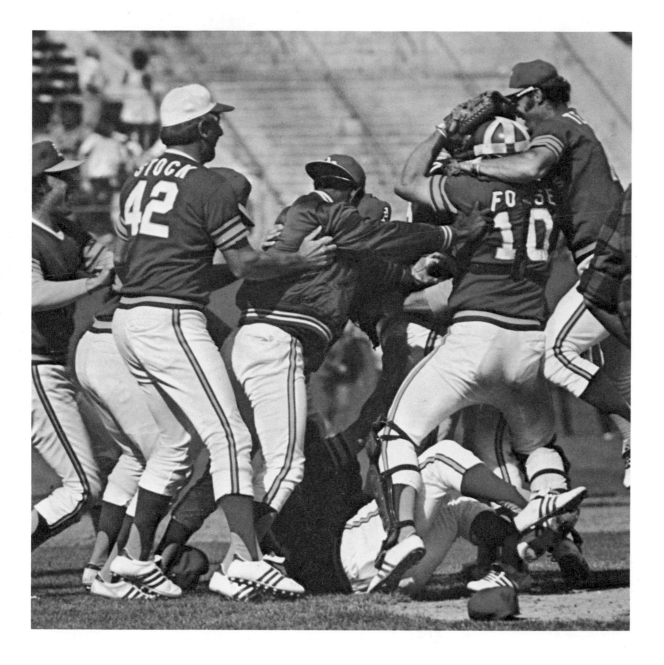

31

Designed by Paul Westermann